Asante Samuel

Carla Mooney
AR B.L.: 6.2 Alt.: 950
Points: 2.0   MG

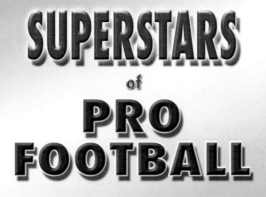

SUPERSTARS
of
PRO
FOOTBALL

ASANTE SAMUEL

Carla Mooney

Mason Crest Publishers

Produced by OTTN Publishing in association with
21st Century Publishing and Communications, Inc.

MASON CREST PUBLISHERS INC.
370 Reed Road
Broomall, Pennsylvania 19008
(866) MCP-BOOK (toll free)
www.masoncrest.com

Printed in the United States of America.

First Printing

9 8 7 6 5 4 3 2 1

Library of Congress Cataloging-in-Publication Data

Mooney, Carla.
    Asante Samuel / Carla Mooney.
        p. cm. — (Superstars of pro football)
    Includes index.
    ISBN 978-1-4222-0542-6 (hardcover) — ISBN 978-1-4222-0836-6 (pbk.)
    1. Samuel, Asante, 1981–   —Juvenile literature. 2. Football players—United States—Biography—Juvenile literature. I. Title.
    GV939.S17M66 2008
    796.332092—dc22
    [B]   2008024186

Publisher's note:
All quotations in this book come from original sources, and contain the spelling and grammatical inconsistencies of the original text.

◀◀ CROSS-CURRENTS ▶▶

In the ebb and flow of the currents of life we are each influenced by many people, places, and events that we directly experience or have learned about. Throughout the chapters of this book you will come across **CROSS-CURRENTS** reference bubbles. These bubbles direct you to a **CROSS-CURRENTS** section in the back of the book that contains fascinating and informative sidebars and related pictures. Go on. ▶▶

◀◀CONTENTS▶▶

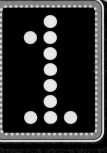

A PRO BOWL PLAYER

In December 2007, the National Football League (NFL) announced the players selected to play in its **prestigious** Pro Bowl. Asante Samuel would start as **cornerback** for the American Football Conference (AFC). It was the first time Asante was selected for the Pro Bowl in his five years with the NFL. Eight of Asante's New England Patriots teammates were also chosen.

Hard Work Pays Off

NFL teams are divided into two conferences, or sections: the AFC and the National Football Conference (NFC). The best players from each conference play in the Pro Bowl, which is the NFL's

Asante Samuel runs with the ball after intercepting a pass, 2007. Thanks to a strong performance during the 2007 season, the Patriots' cornerback was invited to play in the 2008 Pro Bowl in Hawaii.

all-star game. Fans, players, and coaches vote for the players they believe should represent each conference in the game.

CROSS-CURRENTS

If you would like to learn more about the NFL's all-star game, read "History of the Pro Bowl." Go to page 46. ▶▶

Asante was having a fantastic season. At the time of his selection in 2007, he was tied for fourth place for most **interceptions**, with six. He ranked fifth in **passes defended**. Over the past two seasons, Asante led all NFL cornerbacks with 16 interceptions. The Pro Bowl selection was a reward for Asante's hard work. Teammate Rodney Harrison spoke about Asante to *The Boston Globe*:

"Best corner in the league in my opinion. I think week in and week out, people are starting to understand this guy is something special. He's a guy I've seen come from the bottom, who has worked his tail off in the offseason to get to where he's at. He's a guy with tremendous instincts who makes plays everywhere."

The 2007 selection was sweet for Asante. He had not been selected in 2006 for the Pro Bowl, even though that year he had shown his ability to be what players, fans, and sportswriters call a **shutdown cornerback**. In 2006, Asante tied for the NFL lead in interceptions, with 10. He also knocked down 14 passes and made 64 tackles. Many people were surprised Asante was not picked for the Pro Bowl that year, but he used his disappointment as **motivation** to become an even better player.

All-Star Skills

At 5-feet, 10-inches tall and weighing 185 pounds, Asante wasn't the biggest or the fastest player on the field. He became a great player, however, because he knew how to make plays. He was rarely out of position on the field, and he made great adjustments, so receivers couldn't get away from him. He also worked hard at being a good **open-field tackler**, and his great hand-eye coordination allowed him to make interceptions.

Asante's teammates watched him grow from an NFL rookie into a Pro Bowl cornerback. They knew that he had the potential to be a great player. Patriot teammate Tedy Bruschi spoke about Asante:

Asante leaps to pick off a pass during a game against the Buffalo Bills—one of his six interceptions during the 2007 season. Asante's solid defensive play helped the Patriots win all 16 of their regular-season games that year.

"I think he's one of those guys, the minute he came in here we recognized him as a guy that was always getting his hands on balls, whether it's batting down balls or intercepting them. . . . Since Day 1 he's been that type of player, and I think the opportunities are presenting themselves to him in the game now, and he's taking advantage of them, and all of a sudden he has to be looked at as a shutdown corner."

Asante worked hard in the off-seasons and in practice to make himself a better player. He used his instincts on the field to help him make plays. Fellow Patriot Rodney Harrison talked about Asante's hard-working style:

Before Super Bowl XLII, Asante downplayed predictions that the Patriots would win the game. "We just want to go out and play football and not talk about it," the cornerback told the media. "We'll talk about it after the game."

"He wants to get better. He said he wants to be the best corner in the league, and he works at it. So a guy like that you can't teach one thing that he has, and that's instinct. He's always going to be around the ball, no matter if he's playing safety, corner, nickel. . . . He's addicted to football, and that's key."

Asante also had another important quality: confidence. He always felt confident in every play and situation. In an interview with *The Boston Globe*, Asante spoke about the importance of believing in oneself:

"I believe in myself. I believe in my abilities. I know I work hard. I know I understand the game. I can go out there with a little swag, knowing that I can play this position. . . . If you want to be known as one of the greatest to ever play the game, you've got to go out there with a little swag and a little confidence and make plays to back it up."

On the Verge of Greatness

At the time of the Pro Bowl selections, Asante's team, the New England Patriots, had not lost a game. The Patriots stood two wins away from an undefeated regular season. They were driving toward the goals of a Super Bowl win and a perfect season.

With his Pro Bowl selection, Asante proved that he belonged with the **elite** players of the league. The timing couldn't have been better. At the end of the 2007 season, Asante would become a **free agent**.

As a free agent, Asante could **negotiate** a contract with any team in the league. Good cornerbacks were hard to find, and teams were willing to pay well for one. As a Pro Bowl player, Asante was closer than ever to getting a big contract.

The recognition felt good. Over the years, many people had doubted whether Asante had the talent to play in the NFL. He almost wasn't recruited for college football. In the NFL **draft**, team after team passed him by until the Patriots selected him in the fourth round. Asante, however, didn't mind being underrated for most of his career. He'd grown used to working his way up from the bottom.

CROSS-CURRENTS

Check out "Hawaii, Site of the Pro Bowl" to learn more about the place where this annual all-star game is played. Go to page 47.

TOO SMALL, TOO SLOW

Born on January 6, 1981, Asante Samuel was named for the Swahili word meaning "thank you." He was raised by his mother in Fort Lauderdale, Florida, in a community affected by drugs and violence. He watched childhood friends grow wealthy from dealing drugs. Asante, however, kept his eye on a higher prize: a college scholarship.

From an early age, Asante showed a natural athletic talent. At Boyd Anderson High School, Asante played football, baseball, and basketball. Basketball was his first love, but he knew he was too short to play in college. Football was Asante's second choice.

A Slow Quarterback

During his sophomore year of high school, Asante was the football team's quarterback, and he and his top receiver were a potent combination. Asante, however, ran relatively slowly, completing the 40-yard dash in 5.4 seconds. His lack of speed allowed defensive linemen to run him down. At that time, college **scouts** thought he was too small and too slow to play at the college level.

At the end of Asante's junior year, a new coach arrived. Coach Perry Egelsky watched spring drills and made a drastic decision. He announced that he was switching Asante from quarterback to defensive back.

Despite his athletic ability, Asante has worked hard to succeed at football. "I've always been an underrated guy my whole life," he said during a 2007 interview. "I've always had to work my way from the bottom up."

This move angered the team's fans. People called for Egelsky's firing before he'd even coached a game. Asante, too, was upset about the position change. He considered moving to a rival high school.

Coach Egelsky pulled Asante into his office and laid out the truth before him. If Asante wanted to play college football, he needed to switch to defense.

Stubborn Determination

Asante accepted the coach's advice, but he was still not happy. His teammates teased him. They asked how he could stop a receiver if he couldn't even outrun a lineman. These jabs added fuel to Asante's fire. He set out to prove he could be the best.

CROSS-CURRENTS

If you want to learn more about the skills needed to play the cornerback position, read "Defensive Backs." Go to page 48. ▶▶

The summer before his senior year, Asante trained hard. He clipped an Eastbay parachute to his waist and ran sprints. The chute dragged behind and made him feel like he was pulling a 280-pound lineman. Asante also spent time in the weight room using a program designed by Egelsky.

By the end of the summer, Asante had grown two inches and improved his time in the 40-yard dash to 4.85 seconds.

Hard Work, Hard Hits

Asante's hard work paid off. His senior year, he picked off four passes and led the city in pass breakups. He earned All-State honors. Still, Asante needed a good game highlight to show college scouts. That highlight came during a game against Dillard High School.

When a Dillard receiver caught the ball, Asante drilled him hard. The receiver dropped to the field and lay motionless for several minutes. Asante's coach spoke about the play in an interview with *The Boston Globe*:

> **❝He hit him so hard I thought he killed him. The kid's eyes were rolling back in his head. People all over the county still talk about that hit.❞**

The highlight earned Asante the nickname "Asante the Assassin." At his final high school game, the coach grabbed Asante 10 minutes

Athletes sometimes train by sprinting while dragging a parachute. During the summer of 1998, before his senior year at Boyd Anderson High School, Asante used this training method to build up his speed and strength.

before kickoff. The starting quarterback was hurt, and the coach needed Asante to take his place. Asante would be playing on both offense and defense.

It was the opportunity Asante wanted. He had the chance to prove that he could still play quarterback. In the game, Asante threw two touchdown passes and ran for 80 yards. He intercepted two passes and returned punts and kickoffs. Egelsky told *The Boston Globe*:

> **❝It was one of the greatest performances in a single game I've ever seen.❞**

College-Bound

Several college scouts noticed Asante's performance. Eventually, he accepted a scholarship to attend the University of Central Florida.

The University of Central Florida's Asante Samuel (number 28) runs with the ball, 2003. During his college career, Asante had eight interceptions and set a school record by knocking down 38 passes. He also returned punts for the Knights.

In college, Asante continued speed training and weight lifting. His sprint time dropped to 4.6 seconds. By his junior year, Asante and senior Travis Fisher worked as his team's shutdown corners. That year, during the NFL draft, Asante watched the St. Louis Rams select Fisher. Asante talked about his reaction to *The Boston Globe*:

"That's when it clicked. I said to myself, 'I'm better than him. If he can make it, I can make it.'"

Asante finished his senior year with 48 tackles. He also had a team-high 15 pass deflections and four interceptions, and his career total of 38 pass breakups set a school record. His performance earned him an All–Mid-American Conference first-team selection. More importantly, a handful of NFL teams were interested in him.

Draft Day

Asante didn't expect to be picked during the first two rounds of the 2003 draft. He gathered with his family and close friends to watch the draft on television. Asante was nervous, and he couldn't eat the food spread out for the guests.

The Cincinnati Bengals called once to say they were considering Asante for their third-round pick, but Asante watched them choose a receiver instead. By the end of the first day, Asante still hadn't been picked.

The fourth round of the draft began the next day. The Bengals called, but they also passed over Asante. Asante told *The Boston Globe* about his disappointment:

CROSS-CURRENTS

Read "The Language of Football" to learn the meaning of some common football terms and expressions. Go to page 48 ▶▶

"So now I'm stressed really bad. I'm starting to lose it. I'm not eating or nothing. Someone said, 'Maybe the Patriots will take you.' Before the draft, Romeo [Crennel] told me they loved how I hit. But I hadn't heard from them."

Finally, the New England Patriots selected Asante with the 120th pick. His dream of playing in the NFL was about to come true.

TWO RINGS

Asante Samuel couldn't wait to start playing in the NFL. A few weeks after he was picked in the 2003 draft, Asante joined rookie free agents and other Patriots draft picks for a rookie mini-camp. The mini-camp was held at Gillette Stadium in Foxborough, Massachusetts. It was the first official practice of Asante's NFL career.

Camps and Contracts

At mini-camp, Asante took part in agility and position drills and learned to work on special teams. The practices weren't long or difficult, but they served as a good introduction for the new players. Asante knew that he would have to work hard to match the performance of the Patriots' **veteran** players.

A coach gives instructions to rookie cornerback Asante Samuel during his first NFL training camp. Asante's hard work impressed the coaches. "My first training camp with the Patriots I had something like 18 interceptions in practice," he later recalled.

While Asante was working out on the field, his agent was working on Asante's first NFL contract. In mid-July, Asante signed a four-year contract worth $1.7 million. It included a $312,500 signing bonus.

When the Patriots' training camp opened in late July, the corner-back field was crowded. Patriot Pro Bowlers Ty Law and Otis Smith were back to compete for their starting jobs. Asante was part of a group of young players competing for the remaining roster spots.

Asante's spring work had impressed the Patriots' coaches, but they were still concerned that he might have a hard time adjusting to the speed of the NFL. The coaches tapped him to spend time practicing with the starting defensive team.

Asante showed that he could be physical on the field. He played as if nothing could **intimidate** him. Some people didn't expect

In his third NFL game, Asante intercepted a pass from Jets' quarterback Vinnie Testaverde. He ran 55 yards to score his first touchdown as a professional. The fourth-quarter score helped the Patriots win, 23-16.

that type of play from a relatively small player. The Patriots liked Asante's attitude, and he earned a spot on the team. He wasn't the starting cornerback, but he would still receive plenty of playing time.

2003 Season

On September 7, 2003, Asante played in his first NFL game. It was the Patriots' opening game of the season, and they were playing the Buffalo Bills. The game was not a spectacular start for the team. The defense performed poorly and looked **vulnerable** for most of the game. The Patriots lost, 31-0.

After that first game, the Patriots' defense struggled with injuries. In the home opener against the New York Jets, Patriots starter Ty Law injured his ankle. Asante entered the game in his place.

During that game, the Patriots' offense was struggling. They had only scored only one touchdown. The Pats' defense came to the rescue when the Jets were on the New England 43-yard line. Jets quarterback Vinnie Testeverde threw the ball, and Asante stepped in front of the receiver. He intercepted the pass and raced 55 yards for his first NFL touchdown. Asante discussed the play at a press conference:

> **"I had my eyes on the receiver, and then he made his break. When he made his break, then I looked at the quarterback. Actually, [my eyes] lit up because I was looking at the quarterback. I wasn't really concentrating on the ball, but once I tipped it, I was able to make the interception."**

The play sealed a New England win—and earned Asante NFL Rookie of the Week honors.

Week after week, Asante improved as a player. He played in all 16 regular season games, and he finished the season with 34 tackles and two interceptions. The Patriots also improved. Despite their poor start, they finished the season with a record of 14-2 and carried a 12-game winning streak into the playoffs.

Road to the Super Bowl

The Patriots had won the AFC East Division, which earned them a spot in the playoffs. Their first playoff game, against the Tennessee Titans, was tight. The teams were tied at the beginning of the fourth quarter. The Patriots' Pro Bowl kicker, Adam Vinatieri, managed a 46-yard field goal, giving the Patriots a three-point lead.

The Titans, however, still had a chance to win. With a minute and 45 seconds still left in the game, they reached the Patriots' 42-yard line. Titans quarterback Steve McNair threw a pass to Drew Bennett. Asante told *The Boston Globe* what happened next:

> **I just went up for the ball. I was trying to knock the ball down the best I could. I was just going up there trying to make a play.**

He made the play—and broke up the pass. The Patriots won the game!

The Patriots moved on to defeat the Indianapolis Colts in the AFC championship game. Their next stop was Super Bowl XXXVIII.

The Super Bowl against the Carolina Panthers was another tough game. Several players on the Patriots' defense were injured, and Asante was called on to pick up the slack. Carolina quarterback Jake Delhomme took advantage of the Patriots' young players. He completed passes and drove his team into a second-half lead. With nine seconds left in the game, however, Vinatieri kicked a game-winning field goal for New England.

At the end of his first NFL season, Asante had his first Super Bowl ring. It was a prize many NFL players never receive.

CROSS-CURRENTS

For more on the history of the National Football League's championship game, read "The Super Bowl." Go to page 49. ▶▶

Looking for Consistency

The next season, Asante was ready to work. During the 2004 training camp, however, he missed a few days due to an injury. He still wanted the chance to become the starting cornerback. Teammate Rodney Harrison pulled Asante aside to give him some advice. Harrison told *The Boston Globe* what he had told Asante:

> **You have all the talent in the world. You just have to do it day-in, day-out. Sometimes you don't feel like it. Sometimes you feel lazy. When you get in a bad mood, you still have to practice on the same level that you play.**

New England quarterback Tom Brady holds up the Lombardi trophy following the Patriots' 32-29 victory over the Carolina Panthers in Super Bowl XXXVIII, February 1, 2004. The Super Bowl victory was a great finish to Asante's first NFL season.

Coming into camp with a year of experience made a world of difference to Asante. He knew what to expect, and he had a better feel for the game. The coaches noticed his progress. Coach Bill Belichick talked about Asante's performance in training camp:

> **He's one of those guys that gets his hands on a lot of balls. . . . Some guys, it seems like the ball comes to them somehow. They're in the right place, they anticipate things well. They have good reactions and get their hands where the ball's being thrown. He seems like one of those guys.**

Sophomore Season

When the 2004 season began, Asante was still behind veteran starters Ty Law and Tyrone Poole on the team's roster. That would quickly change, however, as the Patriots' defense fell victim to injuries. By the end of October, both starting cornerbacks were on the sidelines.

The Patriots always believed Asante could become an NFL starter. Now it was time for Asante to step up and show them. In an interview with *The Boston Globe*, Asante talked about his role:

> **Here the coach expects that if someone goes down, someone else is supposed to come in and get the job done. Those guys are to do it just as good, if not better. You just have to go out there and play.**

Injuries can happen to any player on any play. Asante was no exception. In early November, on the second play of a game against the St. Louis Rams, Asante collided with a Rams tight end. The hit knocked him out of the game with a shoulder injury. Asante sat out the next game as well. When Asante returned to the field during the following game, an injury struck again, and he was sidelined a few more weeks.

Asante finally came back to play in a game against the Cincinnati Bengals. He immediately made an impact. In the third quarter, Bengals quarterback Carson Palmer tossed a pass down the sideline. Asante intercepted the pass and ran 34 yards for a touchdown. He told *The Boston Globe*:

"I just read the quarterback. It was a three-step drop. I read it, broke on it, and made the play."

By the end of the season, Asante had played in 13 games, with eight starts. In *The Boston Globe*, he talked about the increased game time:

In a December 2004 game against Cincinnati, Asante picked off a pass and scored his second career touchdown. Asante started eight games during the 2004 season. In addition to this interception, he knocked down 12 passes.

> **"I think with each game I learn more and more. Tendencies, you just pick up from being out there. And every game is getting more and more comfortable, so I feel really good about it."**

Critics Silenced

The Patriots were again AFC East Division leaders, and they headed back to the playoffs. There the team faced a stiff challenge against the Indianapolis Colts.

The New England defense was still suffering from injuries. The team even switched receiver Troy Brown to defensive back to fill in for injured players. Asante was only a second-year player, but he was

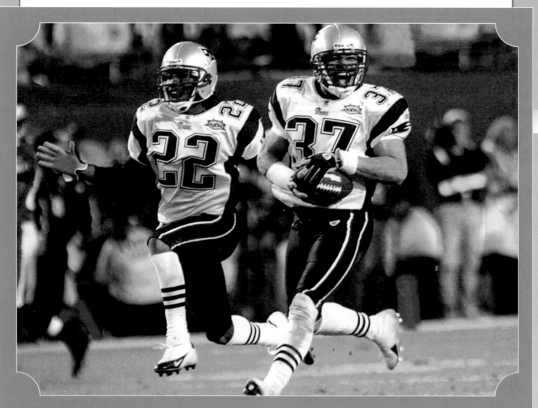

Asante celebrates after teammate Rodney Harrison's interception sealed a 24-21 victory over the Philadelphia Eagles in Super Bowl XXXIX. Asante played a solid game, recording four solo tackles to help the Patriots' defense shut down the Eagles' offense.

now the team's most experienced cornerback. Critics jumped on the defense's inexperience and predicted a post-season disaster.

Asante's experience over the second half of the 2004 season gave him the confidence he needed to face the critics. He told a reporter how doubters affected him:

> **Most definitely it motivates me [when] people are doubting you and think you can't go out and get the job done. [I] just go out there with a little chip on my shoulder and try to prove them wrong.**

The motivation worked for Asante and for the rest of the Patriots' defense. They dismantled Peyton Manning and the Colts, winning 20 to 3. Asante held Colts receiver Marvin Harrison to five catches and 44 yards. It was sweet success. Asante had listened all week to people saying the Patriots couldn't cover the Colts' receivers.

The Patriots beat the Pittsburgh Steelers the following week. They were once again on their way to the Super Bowl.

Another Super Bowl

In Super Bowl XXXIX, the Patriots faced the Philadelphia Eagles. The New England defense set the tone in the first quarter with physical, aggressive play. The Patriots focused on putting pressure on Eagles quarterback Donovan McNabb. They hoped to rattle him early in the game.

On the Eagles' third possession, Asante intercepted a pass. Unfortunately, the play was called back on a penalty.

The two teams struggled back and forth for much of the game. In the end, the Eagles fell short on their final drive, and the Patriots pulled out a 24-21 victory.

For Asante, this second Super Bowl win was **vindication**. He and the other inexperienced defensive players had shown the world they could win the big game.

CROSS-CURRENTS

To see how Asante's Patriots rank among the best teams of all time, read "Football Dynasties." Go to page 50. ▶▶

BREAKOUT PERFORMANCE

When the Patriots' 2005 training camp opened, Asante had a good chance to earn a starting position. Just before camp started, the Patriots released starter Ty Law. The team's other starting cornerback had an off-season knee surgery. It was the opportunity Asante wanted. By the end of the preseason, New England's coaches had decided: Asante would start at cornerback.

Ups and Downs

The 2005 season was rough for the Patriots' defense. Critics knocked them for their **inconsistent** play and for not being able to deliver big plays. In the first half of the regular season, Asante recorded only one interception.

Asante did his best to block out the critics. Week after week, he worked on his performance and learned from his mistakes. He started 15 games, missing a game due to an injury. He led the team with 16 pass knockdowns and recorded 54 tackles, a career high. Asante also finished tied for the team lead in interceptions, with three.

The team finished the season with a record of 10-6. The Patriots won the AFC East Division and earned a playoff spot.

Playoff Performances

In the team's first playoff game after the 2005 season, the Patriots hosted the Jacksonville Jaguars. By the beginning of the fourth quarter, the Jaguars were trailing 21-3, and they were looking to get back in the game.

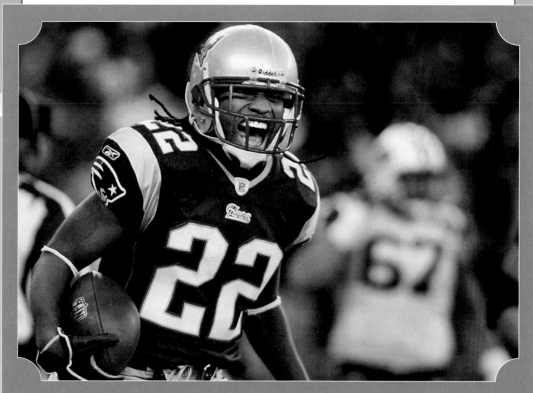

New England's Asante Samuel celebrates after intercepting a pass. During the 2005 season, Asante showed that he was ready to be his team's starting cornerback. In 15 games, he intercepted three passes and knocked down 13 others.

Jacksonville's quarterback threw a pass to his receiver. Asante jumped the route and intercepted the ball. He then raced down the sideline, beating the quarterback to the end zone for a touchdown. Asante talked to *The Boston Globe* about the moment:

"I was reading the quarterback. I saw a man break out, and I kind of baited him into it. I read his eyes and his receivers. It was a go and an out and I just came off my man and took it. . . . Once I caught it and had it, I knew I was going to the house. I wasn't going to let the quarterback catch me. If he would have caught me, man, I would have never heard the end of it, so I knew I had to win."

The New England defense's solid performance against the Jaguars lifted their confidence. They were more aggressive. They went after the quarterback and brought more pressure on the defense.

Unfortunately, the new swagger didn't last long. The next week, the Patriots faced the Denver Broncos, and Denver's offense—along with some questionable calls—were too much for the Patriots to overcome.

Asante was involved in one of the controversial calls. In the second quarter, he raced down the field to cover a Denver receiver. When Asante and the receiver made contact, the officials flagged Asante for pass interference. Many people thought the receiver was at fault and should have been flagged instead.

The penalty gave the Broncos the ball on New England's 1-yard line. Denver soon scored a touchdown and took the lead. Asante intercepted a pass later in the game, but even so, the Patriots were never able to regain the lead.

The Patriots lost 27-13. For the first time in Asante's NFL career, he would not be playing in the Super Bowl.

CROSS-CURRENTS

If you want to learn more about the people who make sure NFL games are played fairly, check out "The Officials." Go to page 52.

Heroics off the Field

Asante was making a difference on the football field, but he also wanted to make a difference off the field. He liked to help people less fortunate than him. Asante spent time working for different charities.

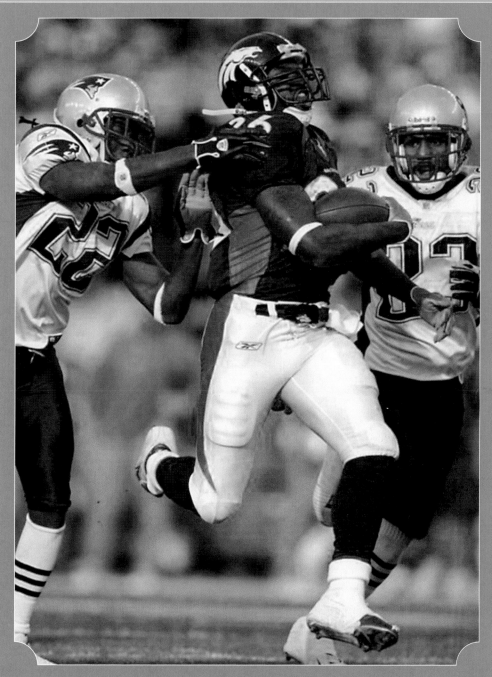

Asante intercepted a pass, knocked down three others, and made three solo tackles during the Patriots' January 2006 playoff game against the Denver Broncos. Despite his solid effort, the Broncos came out on top, 27-13.

He donated time and **memorabilia** to the NFL Charities, and he played with teammates in a fundraiser for a local school. One charity that Asante got involved with was the Book Bank Foundation. This foundation worked to teach children the value of reading and getting an education. Asante donated time, money, and sports memorabilia to the foundation. He also spoke publicly about the charity to make people aware of the work it was doing. In 2006, the foundation recognized the hard work Asante had done for them and gave Asante a Hero Award.

CROSS-CURRENTS

Read "The Book Bank Foundation" to find out about an important children's charity that Asante has helped over the years. Go to page 53. ▶▶

Outstanding Year

Some people believe that in a player's fourth season, the NFL game

During a 2006 game against the Miami Dolphins, Asante picked off two passes, helping the Patriots win, 20-10. Asante had a breakout season in 2006. He finished tied for the most interceptions in the NFL, with 10.

"slows down." This means that the player can see the action more clearly and make better decisions. This was true for Asante.

After the 2005 season, Asante went home for the off-season. He got stronger and put on weight. He also studied films of NFL games to give him insight on what opposing teams might do. He began playing catch with mini footballs to improve his hand-eye coordination and his concentration skills.

The hard work paid off. In 2006, Asante started in 15 games at cornerback. He exploded with 10 interceptions, tied with Champ Bailey for the NFL lead in that category. He led the team with 14 knockdowns and racked up a career-high 64 tackles. In a game against the Chicago Bears, Asante made eight tackles and picked off three passes. For his outstanding play in that game, Asante was named AFC Defensive Player of the Week.

Despite his success on the field, Asante was not the typical outspoken cornerback. He did not trash-talk or dance after every tackle. He rarely boasted in the locker room about his play, even after a good game. Asante didn't enjoy the spotlight. He preferred to let his big hits and interceptions do the talking for him.

Asante's teammates and coaches noticed his growth as a player. Rodney Harrison told *The Boston Globe*:

> **"He's one of the best corners in the league. I keep saying it, but no one's listening. But I think he's making everyone pay attention now. You can just look at his film study, maturation, just growing up and [being] really, really in tune with his body and taking care of himself and really just taking his game to another level."**

In an interview with *The Boston Globe*, Coach Bill Belichick talked about the reasons for Asante's success:

> **"The fundamentals and techniques in the secondary are important. They start in the offseason, and they extend to training camp, and that's what has to carry the players at that position a long way. I think Asante has done a good job of that. . . . He's a smart player. He's instinctive. He has good ball skills."**

Asante's breakout 2006 season could not have come at a better time. It was the final year of his rookie contract. At the end of the season, Asante would become a free agent. He was in a great position to negotiate a new, highly paid contract, but Asante wanted to stay in New England. He hoped a deal could be worked out to keep him with the Patriots.

Asante's agent talked to the Patriots about a contract extension. When his agent and the team's management couldn't agree at first, both sides decided to put the contract on hold and focus on the season.

Disappointments and Motivation

In December 2006, the NFL announced the Pro Bowl selections. Asante's name was not on the list. Despite a great season, Asante had been passed over for a spot on the AFC team. He talked about the snub in *The Boston Globe*:

> **"Of course, being a competitor, I'm disappointed. Life goes on. . . . You just have to go out there and play, and let your play on the field speak for itself."**

His disappointment spilled over into his contract talks with the Patriots. He and the Patriots' management could not agree on how much money Asante should be paid. Asante wanted to be paid like other elite corners in the league. He felt that the offers from the team were disrespectful, so Asante stepped onto the field to make his statement. He would prove his value there.

Back to the Playoffs

The Patriots were in the playoffs again. In the wild card game against the New York Jets, Asante blanketed Jets receivers. He shut down his side of the field for most of the game. Near the end of the game, Asante intercepted a pass from Jets quarterback Chad Pennington and returned it for a touchdown. This was the third postseason interception of his career and the second one that he had returned for a score. The Patriots chalked up another playoff win.

Next, the Patriots traveled across the county to face the San Diego Chargers. The Chargers had the NFL's best record that year, with

Asante breaks up a pass intended for Reggie Wayne of the Colts during a November 2006 game. As Asante developed into a shutdown cornerback, opposing quarterbacks became less likely to throw the ball in his direction.

Quarterback Tom Brady and tight end Daniel Graham celebrate with Asante after he returned an interception 36 yards for a touchdown in a January 2007 playoff game against the Jets. Asante's score sealed the Patriots' 37-16 victory.

14 wins, and the Patriots weren't favored to win the game. Despite being underdogs, the Patriots' defense gave a gritty performance. Patriots quarterback Tom Brady worked fourth-quarter magic to help the team come from behind and win.

The Patriots then headed to the AFC Championship game, a game that determined which team would go to the Super Bowl. This time, the Patriots played the Indianapolis Colts. The Patriots had dominated the Colts in recent years, and the first half of the game proved to be no different. In the second quarter, Indianapolis quarterback Peyton Manning threw a pass to receiver Marvin Harrison. Asante jumped in front of Harrison. He intercepted the pass and returned the ball for a touchdown.

With that play, Asante tied the career NFL playoff record for interceptions returned for a score. Just like that, the Patriots increased their lead to 18 points. It looked as if the Patriots would once again make it to the Super Bowl.

Manning and the Colts, however, would not roll over. The Colts mounted a comeback. With four minutes to go in the third quarter, the game was tied, 21-21. The teams continued to fight back and forth, and the score was locked in a tie two more times. With one minute to go, the Colts took the final lead, 38-34, from a stunned Patriots team.

It was one of the greatest championship game comebacks. This time, however, Asante's team was on the wrong side of the score. Months later, the loss would haunt him. When an ESPN reporter asked Asante if the loss to the Colts still lingered, he replied:

"Yeah, man. It was tough. It was a tough loss. We had it right there in our hands. We just kind of broke down somewhere."

With the season complete, Asante turned his attention to business. His rookie contract was expiring. He wanted a long-term deal with the Patriots.

SUPER BOWL AND SUPER CONTRACT

Asante's spectacular performance during the 2006 season came at the perfect time. His rookie contract was about to expire, and he would become a free agent. He could negotiate a high-paying contract with any team. The Patriots, however, wanted to keep Asante. They felt he was a crucial part of the team, so they put a franchise tag on him.

Franchise Tag

When a team puts a non-exclusive franchise tag on a player, it offers the player a one-year contract. The contract pays the player an average of the previous year's top five salaries for that player's position. The player is still free to talk, or negotiate a different deal, with another team. His team, however, has the right to match any other team's offer and keep the player.

Asante celebrates after scoring a touchdown. When Asante's rookie contract expired after the 2006 season, he hoped that the Patriots would reward him with a new deal worth a lot of money.

Most players don't like the franchise tag. They don't want just a one-year contract; they prefer to sign long-term contracts. Football is a sport where every player is one hit away from injury. A one-year contract is very risky. If a player gets hurt during that year, the player could lose the opportunity to negotiate a new contract.

When the Patriots tagged Asante, they offered him a one-year contract for $7.79 million. Asante was not happy about the tag, but he still hoped he could work out a long-term deal with the Patriots. He began negotiating that contract.

By April 2007, contract talks between Asante and the Patriots broke down. The Patriots were not willing to pay Asante what he thought he was worth. In an interview with the NFL Network, Asante talked about his status:

"I love it here," Asante said early in 2007. "I was born into being a Patriot. I love the guys in the locker room . . . I'm a guy that loves to play football for this team."

"**This is to let everybody know that I'm not happy any-more, and things are not going well. At first I thought it was going well, but it's not. . . . We have a difference of opinion in my value. They think I'm worth one price, and the other teams think I'm worth a lot more. If a long-term deal can't be done at fair numbers for me and New England, then I want to be traded."**

Holding Out

By June 2007, contract talks still had not improved, and Asante refused to sign the one-year deal. Weeks went by without further talks between Asante and the team. The two sides were still far apart in their offers on a long-term contract.

To show his frustration, Asante skipped a **mandatory** mini-camp and backed out of the Patriots' Charitable Foundation Golf Tournament. Asante also threatened to hold out—to not attend training camp or play the start of the regular season.

July 14 was the NFL's deadline for players to sign contract extensions. That day came and went without a deal for Asante. His only options left were to sign the one-year contract or hold out for a better deal.

Asante had a stubborn streak in him. He refused to sign the one-year contract. Without a contract, he did not report to training camp. Finally, at the end of August, a deal was made. Asante signed the one-year contract after the Patriots promised not to place the franchise tag on Asante the next year. The door was open again to keep Asante in New England for the long term.

Asante rejoined the team for the end of training camp and immediately set to work. His previous four years' experience with the Patriots' defense helped him make up the time he missed in camp.

Making a Great Play

Asante's biggest challenge now was getting in shape. Opening day for the 2007 season was in a little more than a week. Asante ran extra conditioning drills to prepare, and in the season opener against the New York Jets, he played well, even though he hadn't played in a single preseason game.

Asante makes an open-field tackle during an October 2007 game against the Dolphins. In 2007, Asante proved that he was one of the NFL's best cornerbacks. He was named to the AFC's Pro Bowl team for the first time.

Within a few weeks, Asante was playing as well as he had in 2006. He often covered the opposing team's top receiver. Quarterbacks recognized his talent, and they threw less often to his side of the field.

By late October, Asante led New England in interceptions and passes defended. He proved that the previous season's success had not been a **fluke**. Asante Samuel was an elite shutdown corner in the NFL.

When the Patriots faced the Philadelphia Eagles in late November 2007, Asante turned in another spectacular performance. He made an interception and returned it for a touchdown. He made a second interception with less than four minutes left in the game. This interception denied the Eagles a score and helped the Patriots win.

By the end of the game, Asante led the team with three passes defended, and he had made three solo tackles. His play earned him AFC Defensive Player of the Week honors. After the game, Asante spoke to reporters:

"That's what it's about. Making plays in the NFL. You never know what kind of game you are going to have. You try to help your team out, going out and playing hard for 60 minutes, and that's what we did."

Hoping to Make History

While Asante achieved personal success, the New England Patriots were on their way to making history. Week after week, the Patriots racked up impressive wins. It wasn't long before the media and fans started talking about whether the Patriots could win all of their games. Only one other team in NFL history had ever won all of its regular season and playoff games—the 1972 Miami Dolphins.

The last game of New England's season was against the New York Giants. Often, teams will rest their starters once they have qualified for postseason play. This way, the players will be fresh for the playoffs. This time, however, both teams sent out their starters for a mighty battle. The Patriots narrowly beat the Giants, 38-35, to finish the regular season with a perfect 16-0 record.

CROSS-CURRENTS

To learn about the only unbeaten team in NFL history, read "The Miami Dolphins Undefeated Season." Go to page 53.

Reporters and fans buzzed around the Patriots. Was this the greatest team of all time? In the middle of this storm, the Associated Press selected Asante to the All-Pro team. The sportswriters recognized his individual performance on a historic team.

The Patriots faced their first two playoff opponents, the Jacksonville Jaguars and San Diego Chargers, with the same **relentless** determination they had displayed all season. They won both games easily. Now, the AFC champion Patriots stood at 18-0, on the brink of their fourth Super Bowl in seven years. The only team standing in their way to making history was the New York Giants, who had managed to win three playoff games on the road to win the NFC title.

Super Bowl Dreams

Super Bowl XLII was the biggest game of the season—and perhaps the biggest game of Asante's career. He knew the stakes, but he believed that great players stepped up for big games.

On February 4, 2008, the Patriots and the Giants met in Glendale, Arizona, for the Super Bowl. The Giants won the opening coin toss. They drove slowly but relentlessly down the field, covering 63 yards in 16 plays. After using up 10 minutes of game time, they kicked a field goal for the first score of the game. The Patriots, however, answered with a touchdown drive and took the lead.

After this score, the Giants' defense continued to swarm the Patriots' offense. They kept New England out of the end zone, and the score remained 7-3 until the fourth quarter. With 11 minutes left in the game, Eli Manning threw a touchdown pass, and the Giants pulled ahead, 10-7.

New England's defense kept New York from scoring again until Patriots quarterback Tom Brady could work his magic. The Pats drove and scored on a quick touchdown pass. They now led 14-10. Less than three minutes stood between the Patriots and a perfect undefeated season.

New York, however, had other plans. With less than three minutes remaining, Giants quarterback Eli Manning led one of the most exciting drives in Super Bowl history. Asante had a chance to end the drive. He leapt up to intercept one of Manning's passes. This time, however, he couldn't come down with the ball. The ball dropped to the turf, and Asante grabbed his head in disbelief.

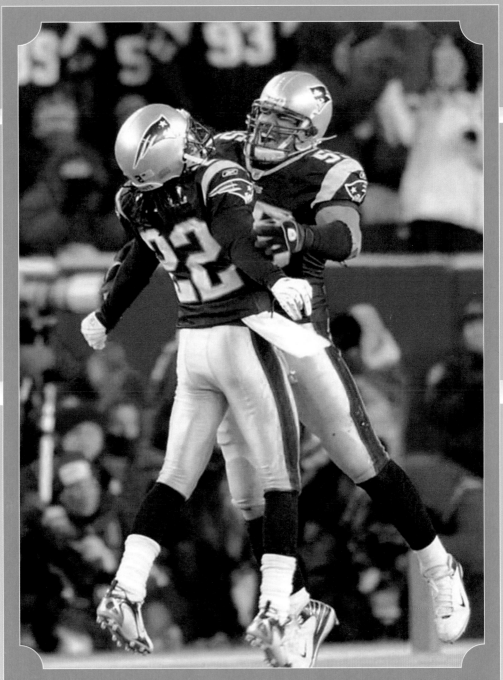

Patriots' linebacker Junior Seau (number 55) celebrates with Asante after the cornerback picked off a pass in the AFC Championship Game, January 20, 2008. The Patriots defeated the San Diego Chargers, 21-12, to advance to the Super Bowl.

Manning then made a huge play. He wiggled out of the grasp of three Patriots and threw a long pass to receiver David Tyree. Tyree jumped for the ball and clasped it against his helmet. He wrestled with a Patriot defender and hung on for the catch. Just a few plays later, Manning tossed a game-winning touchdown pass.

Asante and his teammates were stunned. The Giants, the underdogs, had won, 17-14. It was one of the greatest upsets in Super Bowl history. After the game, Asante spoke to reporters about his missed interception:

CROSS-CURRENTS

Read "Super Bowl Upsets" to find out about other teams that surprised the world to win the NFL's biggest game. Go to page 54. ▶▶

❝I don't know if Eli was trying to throw it away or something. But it was a bad play on my part. I could have ended the game. It was one of the plays that we left on the field, and that is why they are the champions.❞

Moving On

After the season ended, it became clear that Asante and the Patriots were not going to agree on a long-term contract. Asante decided to look at other teams.

The Philadelphia Eagles needed help on defense and believed Asante was the best free agent in the market. They were determined to sign him. Asante wanted to get back to the Super Bowl, and he felt the Eagles gave him a good chance to get there.

On the first day of his free agency, the Eagles gave Asante an offer he couldn't refuse. Asante signed a six-year contract worth $57 million, with $20 million guaranteed. For the first time in his NFL career, Asante would not be a New England Patriot.

Asante was sad to leave the Patriots. He'd grown into a Pro Bowl player with the Patriots, and he had many friends on the team. Asante, however, still looked forward to playing with the Eagles.

Living His Motto

Asante has a tattoo that says "Get Rich To This." Taken from the title of a Gnarls Barkley song, the words hold a special message for Asante. He explained the tattoo to an ESPN reporter:

Asante shows off his new Eagles jersey after signing a six-year, $57 million contract with Philadelphia. He is flanked by Eagles' head coach Andy Reid (left) and team owner Jeff Lurie (right).

"I take it to mean that whatever you're doing—and it's not just about making money—just get rich to this. You're doing your best. You're going all out. You want to succeed and do the best you're doing."

It's a motto that Asante has used throughout his career, and one he hopes to follow for years to come.

History of the Pro Bowl

The Pro Bowl, the NFL's all-star game, takes place a week after the Super Bowl. Since January 1980, the Pro Bowl has been played at Aloha Stadium in Honolulu, Hawaii.

The NFL's all-star game tradition began in 1939. That year, the NFL champions, the New York Giants, defeated a team of all-star players from other teams. This version of the Pro Bowl continued for several years. In 1943, during World War II, the league stopped holding the game.

The NFL brought back the all-star game in 1951. It was now a contest between the best players in the NFL's two conferences. Meanwhile, the rival American Football League (AFL) held its own all-star game. When the NFL and the AFL merged in 1970, the all-star game was officially named the AFC-NFC Pro Bowl.

Coaches, players, and fans vote for the players they think should play in the Pro Bowl. Each group's vote counts as one-third of the total votes. Fans can vote online at the NFL's website. The Pro Bowl's coaches are the coaches of the losing teams in the AFC and NFC conference championships.

In the Pro Bowl, players wear their own team helmets. This practice began in the early 1990s. Before then, AFC players wore a red helmet with a white "A," and NFC players wore a white helmet with a blue "N." (Go back to page 6.) ◀◀

An aerial view of Aloha Stadium in Honolulu, Hawaii, during the 2008 Pro Bowl halftime show. In 2008 Asante Samuel started for the AFC team. He made four tackles during the Pro Bowl.

Hawaii, Site of the Pro Bowl

The Hawaiian islands are located in the Pacific Ocean. Hawaii became a U.S. territory in 1898. In 1959, Hawaii became the 50th state. Today, the population of Hawaii is about 1.2 million.

Hawaii is called the "Aloha State." Six main islands form the state of Hawaii: Kauai, Oahu, Molokai, Lanai, Maui, and the island of Hawaii, which is also known as the Big Island. The history of the Hawaiian Islands goes back centuries.

Over 1,500 years ago, Polynesian settlers sailed over 2,000 miles in canoes and landed on Hawaii's Big Island. Settlers from Tahiti arrived 500 years later. In 1778, British Captain James Cook landed on Kauai. He named the islands the Sandwich Islands, after Great Britain's Earl of Sandwich. After Cook's arrival, other Europeans and Americans came to Hawaii.

Land conflicts among the various groups on the islands were common. In 1791, King Kamehameha united the warring groups on the Big Island. By 1810, he had united all of the Hawaiian Islands under one kingdom.

In 1820, the first Protestant missionaries arrived in Hawaii. Later, seamen, traders, and whalers began using Hawaii as a port. Unfortunately, these visitors brought new diseases to Hawaii. Many of the islands' original peoples became ill or died from these diseases.

By 1893, American settlers controlled a large portion of Hawaii's economy. In a peaceful **coup**, the settlers overthrew the Hawaiian Kingdom. In 1898, the United States added Hawaii as a territory. It became the 50th state of the United States in 1959. (Go back to page 9.) ◀◀

Defensive Backs

The name *defensive back* can refer to either safeties or cornerbacks. Defensive backs are also known as the "secondary," since they take positions behind the players on the defensive line.

Defensive backs often have the most difficult job in football. They have to cover speedy receivers. They are the last line of defense on both running and pass plays. If an opponent runs past a defensive back, that opponent has a good chance of scoring.

On running plays, the defensive back must find the player carrying the ball and move quickly to make a tackle. On passing plays, the defensive back either covers a certain receiver ("man-to-man" coverage) or a particular area of the field (a "zone" defense). The defensive back tries to deflect or intercept the ball before the receiver catches it. If the receiver does catch the ball, the defensive back tries to make a tackle. He wants to prevent the receiver from gaining more yards on the play.

Defensive backs need to be fast to keep up with wide receivers. They also must have good tackling skills and good hand-eye coordination. They need to see the ball in the air and be able to reach out and intercept a pass. Some NFL defensive backs played as receivers in high school or college. (Go back to page 12.) ◀◀

The Language of Football

down: a period of game time that starts when the ball is put into play, or becomes "live," and ends when the ball is taken out of play, or is "dead." Each team gets four downs to move the ball 10 yards or more.

encroachment: a penalty that occurs when a player enters the neutral zone and makes contact with an opponent before the ball is snapped.

fumble: to lose possession of the ball.

loose ball: a live ball not in the possession of any player.

neutral zone: the area between two imaginary lines extending out on either side from the ends of the ball, when the ball is placed on the field before a down. The offense and defense must stay behind these lines. The offensive player who snaps the ball is the only player allowed to be in the neutral zone.

offside: a penalty that occurs when any part of a player's body is beyond the scrimmage line when the ball is snapped.

possession: having control of the ball, with at least both feet or another part of a player's body (except the hands) on the ground inbounds.

punt: the act of kicking the ball away to the opposing team on the fourth down after the offense has failed to move the ball 10 yards within three downs.

safety: a score that occurs when a defensive player tackles an offensive player in the offense's own end zone. In a safety, the defense scores two points and then becomes the receiving team on a kick-off.

sudden death: a type of overtime play that occurs when two teams are tied at the end of the fourth quarter. The first team to score during sudden death play wins the game.

(Go back to page 15.) ◀◀

The Super Bowl

The first Super Bowl was played as part of a merger agreement between the National Football League (NFL) and the American Football League (AFL). It was originally named the AFL-NFL World Championship Game, but within a few years, the catchier name "Super Bowl" had become official.

The Green Bay Packers and the Kansas City Chiefs played in the first Super Bowl in 1967, and the Packers won. The Packers also won the second Super Bowl in 1968. The AFL did not win its first Super Bowl until Super Bowl III. That year (1969), Joe Namath's New York Jets upset the Baltimore Colts, 16-7.

In 1970, the AFL and NFL merged into one league, the NFL. The NFL teams were then split into two conferences, the National Football Conference (NFC) and the American Football Conference (AFC). Now the best team from each conference plays in the Super Bowl.

The winning Super Bowl players and coaches each receive a Super Bowl ring, and the team receives the Vince Lombardi Trophy. Vince Lombardi was the coach of the Green Bay Packers when they won the first two Super Bowls. After Lombardi's death, the NFL named the Super Bowl trophy in his honor. (Go back to page 20.) ◀◀

The Vince Lombardi Trophy is awarded each year to the team that wins the Super Bowl. It was named for legendary Green Bay Packers head coach Vince Lombardi, whose teams won the first two Super Bowls.

Football Dynasties

In January 2005, by winning their third Super Bowl in four years, the New England Patriots established themselves as one of NFL's great **dynasties**. Take a look at other dynasties of the last four decades of the 20th century.

The Green Bay Packers of the 1960s. In the 1960s under legendary coach Vince Lombardi, the Pack won five pro championships in seven years. These championships included the last pre-merger NFL Championship game in 1966 and the first two AFL-NFL Super Bowls, in 1967 and 1968. Packer greats of the Lombardi era included quarterback Bart Starr, running backs Jim Taylor and Paul Hornung, offensive lineman Jerry Kramer, linebacker Ray Nitzschke, safety Willie Wood, and cornerback Herb Adderley. Many of those Packers were eventually elected to the Pro Football Hall of Fame.

The Pittsburgh Steelers of the 1970s. For most of their history, Pittsburgh was one of the worst pro football teams, unable to win an NFL championship. That changed during the 1970s, when the Steelers won four Super Bowl titles in six years. They faced stiff competition from tough Cowboys and Raiders teams during that decade. The Steelers produced great players like defensive lineman Charles "Mean Joe" Greene, linebackers Jack Ham and Jack Lambert, quarterback Terry Bradshaw, wide receivers Lynn Swann and John Stallworth, and running back Franco Harris. Ten Steelers from those 1970s teams, including Coach Chuck Noll, have earned places in the Pro Football Hall of Fame.

The San Francisco 49ers of the 1980s. The 49ers won four Super Bowls thanks to the performances of Hall of Fame quarterback Joe Montana. One of the greatest clutch performers in the history of the NFL, Montana led his team to victories in Super Bowl XVI (1982), XIX (1985), XXIII (1989), and XXIV (1990). Montana's main target was wide receiver Jerry Rice; other San Francisco stars included wide receiver Dwight Clark, running back Roger Craig, and defensive back Ronnie Lott. The 49ers remained a top team into the 1990s, and won a fifth Super Bowl in 1995 with Steve Young at quarterback.

The Dallas Cowboys of the 1990s. During the 1990s, the Cowboys won three Super Bowls in four years (XXVII, in 1993; XXVIII, in 1994; and XXX, in 1996). On offense, the core of the team was quarterback Troy Aikman, running back Emmitt Smith, and wide receiver Michael Irvin.

(Go back to page 25.) ◀◀

Patriots quarterback Tom Brady (number 12) prepares to lead the team onto the field before a game. The Patriots' Super Bowl victories in 2002, 2004, and 2005 ensured the team's place as one of the greatest NFL dynasties.

The Officials

Every NFL game uses seven officials: the referee, the umpire, the head linesman, the line judge, the field judge, the side judge, and the back judge. Each official has a specific job, and some officials cover specific parts of the field. Officials wear black-and-white striped shirts, to distinguish themselves from the players' colorful jerseys.

The referee is the official who oversees the overall game. He starts the game by conducting the coin toss. When rules are broken during the game, the referee signals to indicate what happened and explains the penalty to the crowd. The referee also judges instant replays and has the last say on rule interpretations.

The umpire stands on the defensive side of the line of scrimmage—right in the middle of the action. He watches the defensive and offensive linemen for false starts, illegal blocks, or holding.

The head linesman stands near the line of scrimmage at the start of each play. He watches for players who accidentally move across the line of scrimmage before the ball is snapped—this is called "offsides" or "encroachment." The head linesman also rules on out-of-bounds calls on his side of the field and watches receivers for holding and illegal blocks. The head linesman marks the ball's position after each play, and is in charge of the crew that measures for first downs.

The line judge lines up opposite the linesman and rules on the same plays. The line judge also decides whether the quarterback is behind the line of scrimmage when he passes the ball.

The field judge works on one side of the defensive secondary, watching receivers, running backs, and defensive backs to make sure they don't illegally block or hold other players. He makes sure players stay in bounds, that their catches are legal, and that there is no pass interference. The field judge also rules whether field goal attempts and **point conversions** are successful.

The side judge has the same responsibilities as the field judge, but the side judge is on the opposite side of the field.

The back judge stands 25 yards downfield, and watches for bad blocks, holding, illegal use of the hands, and pass interference. Like the field judge, the back judge also rules on field goals and point conversions. (Go back to page 28.) ◀◀

The Book Bank Foundation

Entertainment manager and sports agent Glenn Toby founded the Book Bank Foundation in 1997. The foundation's goal is to teach children the values of reading and getting a good education. Toby knows these values first hand.

When Toby was young, he and his family were homeless for eight years. During that time, reading was a way for Toby to escape his hard life. He created the Book Bank Foundation to help other children in need, particularly homeless children and children in the nation's inner cities.

The foundation has many programs. Education, health, and relationship seminars reach out to youth at risk. Some sessions help boost a child's self-esteem. Other sessions give real life examples of what can happen without an education. The foundation sends books and magazines to schools that need supplies.

The foundation also works with adults, teaching adults how to get children excited about reading and learning. The foundation offers tutoring and career counseling, and it organizes clothing and medicine drives for the homeless.

Glenn Toby believes that every child should have a fair chance to turn his or her life around. The Book Bank Foundation works every day to give children that chance. (Go back to page 30.) ◀◀

The Miami Dolphins' Undefeated Season

In 1972, the Miami Dolphins achieved a perfect season. They were the first team in the National Football League to finish a season without a loss or a tie.

That year, the Dolphins were coached by Don Shula. It was his third year coaching the Dolphins, and Shula shaped his players into a great team.

Future Hall of Fame players Nick Buoniconti, Larry Csonka, Larry Little, Bob Griese, Jim Langer, and Paul Warfield led the team. Many other players, however, were not well known. This lack of stars earned Miami's defense the nickname "No-Name Defense."

The Dolphins were able to perform well even after losing their starting quarterback. In week five, quarterback Bob Griese went down with an injury, and backup quarterback Earl Morrall stepped into the starting spot. Morrall managed to keep the team on its winning streak.

The Dolphins finished the regular season without a loss. In the playoffs, they won two tough games, one against the Cleveland Browns and one against the Pittsburgh Steelers. In Super Bowl VII, the Dolphins beat the Washington Redskins to complete a perfect season.

No team has ever matched Miami's record. Several teams, including the Patriots, have come close, but all have fallen short. Each year, football fans are left to wonder if this will be the year their team will have a perfect season. (Go back to page 41.) ◀◀

Super Bowl Upsets

The New York Giants' 17-14 win over the previously unbeaten Patriots in February 2008 is considered one of the biggest upsets in Super Bowl history. However, the Giants were not the first underdogs to win a Super Bowl. In several other Super Bowls, teams defied expectations to pull off the unthinkable:

New York Jets in Super Bowl III (1969). The NFL's Green Bay Packers had won the first two Super Bowls convincingly over the AFL's Kansas City Chiefs and Oakland Raiders. By Super Bowl III, many people wondered whether an AFL team could ever win a Super Bowl against an NFL team. That would change after Super Bowl III. On the Thursday before the game, Joe Namath, quarterback of the AFL champion New York Jets, told the press he "guaranteed" that his team would defeat the Baltimore Colts. The Colts had the league's best defense, and one of its best offenses, so most people laughed at this prediction. However, the Jets dominated the Colts throughout the game, and Namath's cocky guarantee became legendary. He was chosen as the game's outstanding player.

Denver Broncos in Super Bowl XXXII (1998). Before 1998, the Denver Broncos had gone to the Super Bowl four times—and lost every time. Many people believed Broncos quarterback John Elway couldn't win the big game. In Super Bowl XXXII, the Broncos faced the Green Bay Packers and quarterback Brett Favre. Green Bay had defeated New England in the previous year's Super Bowl, and few expected the Broncos to beat this tough team. In the final two minutes of the game, however, Elway drove the Broncos to a game-winning touchdown. The long-time underdogs finally won the Lombardi Trophy.

New England Patriots in Super Bowl XXXVI (2002). The St. Louis Rams' high-scoring offense was called the "Greatest Show on Turf," and before the game the Patriots were expected to lose by two touchdowns. However, the Patriots stayed in the game thanks to strong play by their defense, which forced the Rams to turn over the ball three times. With the score tied at 17-17, and less than two minutes left, New England quarterback Tom Brady led his team down the field. In the final seconds, Adam Vinateri kicked a field goal to win the game. This was the Patriots' first Super Bowl title.

(Go back to page 44.) ◀◀

1981 Asante Samuel is born on January 6 in Fort Lauderdale, Florida.

1998 In his final year of high school, Asante earns All-State and All-County honors as a defensive back.

1999 Asante attends college at the University of Central Florida.

2001 As a junior, Asante is an All-Independent first-team selection.

2002 Asante receives All–Mid-American Conference first-team selection in his senior year.

2003 The New England Patriots draft Asante as the 120th overall pick.

Asante is named NFL Rookie of the Week for his game against the New York Jets on September 21.

2004 Asante and the New England Patriots win Super Bowl XXXVIII on February 1.

2005 The New England Patriots become Super Bowl champions once more. They win Super Bowl XXXIX on February 6.

2006 Asante is named AFC Defensive Player of the Week for his game against the Chicago Bears on November 26.

The Book Bank Foundation selects Asante as a Hero Award recipient.

2007 The Patriots place the franchise tag on Asante.

Asante is named AFC Defensive Player of the Week for his game against the Philadelphia Eagles on November 25.

Asante is selected as a starter for the AFC Pro Bowl team.

Asante earns first-team All Pro honors from the Associated Press.

2008 In a stunning upset, the Patriots lose Super Bowl XLII to the New York Giants on February 3.

Asante signs a contract with the Philadelphia Eagles.

Regular Season Statistics

Year	Team	G	ST	AT	TT	PD	Int	Yds	Avg	Long	TD
2003	NE	16	30	4	34	5	2	55	27.5	55t	1
2004	NE	13	34	2	36	11	1	34	34.0	34t	1
2005	NE	15	44	10	54	16	3	15	5.0	15	0
2006	NE	15	59	5	64	14	10	120	12.0	33	0
2007	NE	16	41	3	44	18	6	89	14.8	42	1

Key
G: games
ST: solo tackles
AT: assisted tackles
TT: total tackles
PD: passes defended
Int: interceptions
Yds: yards returned
Avg: average yards returned per interception
Long: longest interception return (t indicates a score)
TD: touchdowns scored

Awards

1998   All-State (Florida) and All-County (Broward) honors

2001   All-Independent first-team selection

2002   All–Mid-American Conference first-team selection

2003   NFL Rookie of the Week (September 21)

2006   AFC Defensive Player of the Week (November 26)

Book Bank Foundation Hero Award

2007   AFC Defensive Player of the Week (November 25)

NFL Pro Bowl; All-Pro selection (Associated Press)

Books and Periodicals

Benjamin, Amalie. "Samuel Had Book on Excellent Reads." *The Boston Globe* (Oct. 9. 2006), E7.

Boston Globe, ed. *Driven: The Patriots' Ride to a Third Title*. Chicago: Triumph Books, 2005.

Boston Herald. New England Patriots: 2004 Super Bowl Champs. Boston: Sports Publishing, 2004.

Holley, Michael. *Patriot Reign: Bill Belichick, the Coaches, and the Players Who Built a Champion*. New York: HarperCollins Publishers, 2005.

MacMullan, Jackie. "Payment Due." *The Boston Globe* (Jan. 7, 2007), C1.

Wilson, Tom, and Rippey, Paul, editors. *Patriotology Trivia Challenge: New England Patriots Football*. Columbus, OH: Kick the Ball, Ltd., 2008.

Web Sites

http://www.philadelphiaeagles.com

The official Web site of the Philadelphia Eagles has Asante's biography, year-by-year statistics, and career highlights.

http://www.patriots.com

The official Web site of the New England Patriots includes game recaps, player biographies, schedules, news, and more.

http://www.nfl.com

The Web site of the National Football League includes schedules, statistics, team news, Super Bowl history and more.

http://www.thebbf.org

The Book Bank Foundation's Web site includes information on programs and how to get involved.

http://www.espn.com

ESPN has the latest sports and player news, scoreboards, scoring, and schedules.

cornerback—a member of the defensive team's backfield whose main job is to intercept or cause incomplete passes thrown by the opposing team. His job is also to tackle ball carriers.

coup—the sudden overthrow of a group that holds power.

draft—the process by which NFL teams select new team members from the nation's top college football players.

dynasties—groups of people who maintain positions of power or leadership for a long time.

elite—the best of a class or group.

fluke—a stroke of luck.

free agent—an athlete who is not contracted by or committed to playing for a specific team and who can negotiate a contract with any team.

inconsistent—not showing a regular pattern.

interception—the stealing, or pick-off, of a pass, usually thrown by the quarterback, by a member of the opposing team's defense.

intimidate—make timid or fearful.

mandatory—required.

memorabilia—objects, such as autographs, balls, or jerseys, that serve as reminders of certain well-known people or events.

motivation—a reason for a person to take action.

negotiate—to talk with another person or group to settle a matter or disagreement.

open-field tackler—a defensive player—usually a member of the backfield—whose job is to tackle a ball carrier who has made it through the defensive linemen and possibly prevent that ball carrier from scoring.

pass defended—also called a pass deflected, an incomplete pass caused by a defender's slapping down or otherwise deflecting the pass and preventing it from being caught.

point conversions—adding one or two extra points to the score after a touchdown is made. Point conversions are made by running or passing the ball into the end zone or kicking the ball through the upright poles of the goal post.

prestigious—seen as valuable by many people.

relentless—showing no lessening in strength or pace.

scout—a person who works for a specific team and looks for talented athletes to play on that team.

shutdown cornerback—a term used to describe a cornerback who is so good at his job of defending against pass plays that the opposing team avoids throwing the ball anywhere near him.

veteran—a person with experience.

vindication—the act of proving somebody to be correct and justified.

vulnerable—open to attack or damage.

page 6 "Best corner in the league . . ." Reiss, Mike. "Bowl Game: Patriots Get 8." *The Boston Globe* (Dec. 19, 2007) D1.

page 8 "I think he's one . . ." Ramsey, Ethan. "Samuel Keeps on Proving His Value." *The Boston Globe* (Oct. 23, 2006) D5.

page 8 "we just want to go . . ." Mark Cannizzaro, "Pats' Reaction to Burress: talk is Cheap," *New York Post* (January 30, 2008). http://www.nypost.com/seven/01302008/sports/giants/pats__reaction_to_burress__talk_is_cheap_905397.htm

page 9 "He wants to get better . . ." Benjamin, Amalie. "Samuel Had Book on Excellent Reads." *The Boston Globe* (Oct. 9 2006) E7.

page 9 "I believe in myself . . ." Gasper, Christopher L. "He Has Free Agency Cornered." *The Boston Globe* (Nov. 30, 2007) E7.

page 11 "I've always been . . ." Jeff Cournoyer, "Q&A with CB Asante Samuel," Patriots.com (January 12, 2007). http://www.patriots.com/search/index.cfm?ac=searchdetail&pid=23691&pcid=41&rss=1

page 12 "He hit him so hard . . ." MacMullan, Jackie. "Payment Due." *The Boston Globe* (Jan. 7, 2007) C1.

page 14 "It was one of the . . ." MacMullan, "Payment Due," C1.

page 15 "That's when it clicked . . ." MacMullan, "Payment Due," C1.

page 15 "So now I'm stressed . . ." MacMullan, "Payment Due," C1.

page 17 "My first training camp . . ." Cournoyer, "Q&A with CB Asante Samuel."

page 19 "I had my eyes . . ." Perillo, Paul. "Patriots Persevere in Home Opener." *Patriots Football Weekly* (Sept. 24, 2003). http:///www.pfwonline.com.

page 20 "I just went up . . ." Blaudschun, Mark. "Jarring Finish for Bennett." *The Boston Globe* (Jan. 11, 2004) C3.

page 20 "You have all the talent . . ." Kilgore, Adam. "Samuel Turning Corner." *The Boston Globe* (Aug. 19, 2004) C7.

page 22 "He's one of those guys . . ." Kilgore, "Samuel Turning Corner," C7.

page 22 "Here the coach expects . . ." Burris, Joe. "He's Got It Covered." *The Boston Globe* (Nov. 6, 2004) D1.

page 23 "I just read the . . ." Cafardo, Nick. "A Qualified Success." *The Boston Globe* (Dec. 13, 2004) D1.

page 24 "I think with each game . . ." Burris, "He's Got It Covered," D1.

page 25 "Most definitely it motivates . . ." Tadych, Frank. "Patriots Notebook: Samuel Hears Critics." *Patriots. Com.* 20 Jan. 2005. 21 Apr. 2008. http://www.patriots.com/news/index.cfm?ac=generalnewsdetail&pcid=47&pid=10523.

page 28 "I was reading the . . ." Gasper, Christopher L. "Samuel Picks His Moment to Step Up." *The Boston Globe* (Jan. 8, 2006) C3.

page 31 "He's one of the best . . ." Ramsey, "Samuel Keeps on Proving His Value," D5.

page 31 "The fundamentals and techniques . . . " MacMullan, "Payment Due," C1.

page 32 "Of course, being . . . " Reiss, Mike. "Patriots are Motivated Speakers." *The Boston Globe* (Dec. 21, 2006) D1 2.

page 35 "Yeah, man. It was tough . . . " Hill, Jemele. "Riding with...Asante Samuel." *ESPN.Com*. 17 July 2007. 21 Apr. 2008 http:// sports.espn.go.com/espn/ page2/story?page=hill/070716.

page 38 "I love it here . . ." Cournoyer, "Q&A with CB Asante Samuel."

page 39 "This is to let everybody . . . " Reiss, Mike. "Samuel Eyes Trade." *The Boston Globe* (Apr. 5, 2007) E1.

page 41 "That's what it's about . . . " "Patriots Postgame Quotes" *Patriots.Com*. 25 Nov. 2007. 2 May 2008

page 44 "I don't know if . . . " Vega, Michael. "Defense Didn't Convert Save." *The Boston Globe* (Feb. 4, 2008) E6.

page 45 "I take it to mean . . . " Hill, "Riding with . . . Asante Samuel."

Numbers in ***bold italics*** refer to captions.

Carla Mooney is a freelance writer who has written two books and numerous magazine articles for young readers. She lives outside of Pittsburgh, Pennsylvania, with her husband and three children.

PICTURE CREDITS